An Angel Came to Nazareth

For Michelle—M. K.

For Rosemary—A. D. K.

An Angel Came to Nazareth

Written by
Anthony Knott

With pictures by Maggie Kneen

SCHOLASTIC INC.
New York Toronto London Auckland Sydney
Mexico City New Delhi Hong Kong Buenos Aires

An Angel

came to Nazareth

Upon a winter's day
And there she spied four animals
At breakfast on the hay.

"Camel, donkey, horse, or ox,
"Just one beast from this stall
Will carry into Bethlehem
The greatest of them all."

An Angel came to Nazareth

Upon a winter's day

And there she spied four travelers

To help upon their way.

"Each beast must choose," the angel said,
"His burden big or small,
For among them one will carry
The greatest of them all."

"I will choose,"
the proud horse cried,
"The soldier strong and tall.
So valiant and good is he,
He must be best of all."

"He's strong and tall," the angel said,
"A mighty man is he,
And many valiant deeds he'll do,
But not the greatest be."

"I will choose,"
the strong ox cried,
"In my cart to haul,
The goodly, kind Samaritan.
He must be best of all."

"He's kind and good," the angel said,
"A helpful man is he,
And many selfless deeds he'll do,
But not the greatest be."

"I will choose," the camel cried,
"Not to let this wise man fall,
For following a
wondrous star,
He must be best of all."

"He's wise and just," the angel said,
"A goodly king is he,
And he shall find what that star means,
But not the greatest be."

"Now I will choose," the donkey cried,
"Not good or great or tall,
but the lady waiting here
Who needs bearing most of all."

"Then you must take,"
the angel said,
"Your burden preciously
For she herself a burden bears
That shall the greatest be."

To Bethlehem,
to Bethlehem,

We must not stop or stray,
But with a star to guide us
We shall not lose the way.

To Bethlehem, to Bethlehem,
The miles are hard and long.
But good shepherds point the way
And we'll be there anon.

An angel came to Bethlehem,
On that first Christmas morn
And cried, "Of all the travelers,
The best, this donkey's borne."

He carried Mary gently
And brought her to this stall,
Where Jesus Christ,
Her child is born,
The greatest of them all!"

ISBN-13: 978-0-439-91195-5
ISBN-10: 0-439-91195-8

Published by Scholastic Inc., 557 Broadway, New York, NY 10012,
by arrangement with Chronicle Books.

12 11 10 9 8 7 6 5 4 3 2 1 6 7 8 9 10 11/0

Printed in the U.S.A. 40

First Scholastic printing, November 2006

Book design by Janie Louise Hunt.

Typeset in Galahad.

The illustrations in this book were rendered in watercolor and gouache.